The Nature Kid's Guide to
FERRETS

DAVID ANDERSON

LP Media Inc. Publishing

For information address LP Media Inc. Publishing,
30012 Variolite St NW, Princeton MN 55371
www.lpmedia.org

Publication Data

Ferrets
The Nature Kid's Guide to Ferrets — First edition.

Summary: "Learn all about Ferrets, the Nature Kid Way"
— Provided by publisher.

ISBN: 979-8-89818-170-3

[1. Ferrets – Non-Fiction] I. Title.

Title: The Nature Kid's Guide to Ferrets

CONTENTS

PRAIRIE PATROL

Pop! A black-footed ferret pokes its masked face out of the ground. Its dark eyes scan the open grassland.

Black-footed ferrets are America's only wild ferret. They live on the wide, flat grasslands called the Great Plains. The sky is huge and the grass grows short.

These ferrets need open land with soft soil. The ground must be easy to dig. They cannot live in forests, mountains, or swamps.

Underground **burrows** are their home. Tunnels stay cool in summer and warm in winter. A good burrow has many rooms and several ways in and out.

FERRET FINDS

Wyoming has the largest population of black-footed ferrets. The Shirley Basin site near Medicine Bow is home to the most animals.

Crunch! A ferret crosses a patch of dry grass. It moves between burrows on the open plain.

Black-footed ferrets once lived across 12 U.S. states. Their range stretched from Canada all the way south to Mexico. Millions of prairie dogs filled the land, and ferrets thrived.

Then farmers poisoned prairie dogs to protect crops. When the prairie dogs vanished, so did the ferrets. By 1979, people believed black-footed ferrets were gone forever.

In 1981, a ranch dog in Wyoming found a dead ferret. That discovery led to a small surviving group nearby. Today, ferrets live at about 30 protected sites across the western United States.

SMALL BUT MIGHTY

A black-footed ferret can stretch its body up to 30 percent longer when squeezing through tight underground tunnels.

Stretch! A black-footed ferret presses its long body flat against the earth.

Black-footed ferrets are small but built for action. Adults grow 18 to 24 inches long from nose to tail. Males weigh about 1.5 to 2.5 pounds. Females are lighter.

Their bodies are long and thin like a tube. From the neck to the hips, they stay almost the same width. This lets them slide through prairie dog tunnels with ease.

They stand only 4 to 5 inches tall at the shoulder. But do not be fooled by their size. These little hunters are fast, strong, and tough.

MASKED MARVEL

The black-footed ferret has a third eyelid that helps protect its eyes while digging underground.

Peek! A black-footed ferret stops at the burrow entrance. That dark mask makes it easy to recognize.

Black-footed ferrets have a look all their own. A bold black mask covers their eyes like a bandit. Their body fur is pale yellow to tan. Their feet, lower legs, and tail tip are sooty black.

They have 34 sharp teeth built for eating meat. Their long canine teeth grip and hold prey tight.

Large front paws have strong curved claws for digging. Their spine is very flexible. Small, rounded ears sit high on their heads. Long whiskers help them feel in the dark.

SUPER SNIFFERS

Black-footed ferrets make many sounds. They chatter as an alarm call, hiss when afraid, and chirp to talk to their young kits.

12

Sniff! A ferret raises its nose to the air. Something is stirring down below.

The black-footed ferret's best sense is smell. It can detect a sleeping prairie dog deep underground in the dark. Scientists believe smell is the most important tool for hunting.

Ferrets also see well in low light. This helps them hunt at night. But they cannot see bright colors clearly.

Their hearing is sharp too. They pick up high sounds that humans cannot hear. Long whiskers help them feel small air movements. This is very useful in tight, dark tunnels where sight does not work well.

BEST FRENEMIES

Bark! A prairie dog calls out a warning. But it may already be too late.

The black-footed ferret cannot survive without the prairie dog. Prairie dogs make up 90 percent of a ferret's diet. They are the perfect meal.

Prairie dogs also build the burrows where ferrets sleep and raise their young. Ferrets move into empty tunnels and take them over.

One ferret family needs more than 250 prairie dogs per year just to survive. This means they need large, healthy prairie dog towns nearby. If the prairie dogs disappear, the ferrets cannot live.

MEAT EATERS

A black-footed ferret uses its long whiskers to feel its way through dark underground tunnels, sensing every twist and turn without using its eyes at all!

Zoom! A black footed ferret chases a mouse at dusk. But it escapes down a small hole.

Black-footed ferrets are **carnivores**. They only eat meat. Their bodies cannot digest fruits or plants.

Prairie dogs are their main food. But ferrets also eat mice, ground squirrels, and rabbits when they can find them. Nearly everything they eat lives underground or close to it.

One ferret eats about one prairie dog every three or four days. That adds up to more than 100 prairie dogs in a single year.

Ferrets hunt mostly at night. They may search many burrows before they find their meal.

TUNNEL HUNTERS

Black-footed ferrets can travel up to five miles in a single night while hunting!

Slip! The ferret vanishes into a dark hole. The underground hunt has begun.

Black-footed ferrets hunt at night. Their long, thin bodies slide into prairie dog burrows with ease. This is where sleeping prairie dogs are found.

Inside the tunnel, they use smell to find their prey. When they locate it, they strike hard and fast with a bite to the throat.

One ferret may check many burrows in a single night. They cover a lot of ground on their nightly hunts.

QUICK ESCAPE

Whoosh! The ferret sprints to its burrow just before danger arrives.

Black-footed ferrets have many ways to stay safe. Their pale fur blends into dry grass and soil. It is hard to spot them from above.

When danger comes near, ferrets run fast. They can reach 15 miles per hour. They bound between burrow entrances in short, quick bursts.

If they cannot outrun a predator, they dive underground. Narrow tunnels protect them from most enemies who cannot follow. Ferrets also release a bad-smelling **musk** from glands near their tail. This surprise can buy them time to escape.

WATCH OUT!
FUN FACT!
Golden eagles can spot prey from over a mile away!
22

Screech! A golden eagle circles overhead. The ferret freezes at the burrow entrance.

Black-footed ferrets have many enemies. Golden eagles and great horned owls hunt them from the sky. These birds have sharp eyes and can spot a ferret from far away.

On the ground, coyotes and badgers are a danger. Badgers can dig into burrows to find them. Rattlesnakes can slide right into tunnels.

Ferrets are most active at night. This helps them avoid eagles and hawks. But owls and coyotes also hunt in the dark. There is always a risk when they come above ground.

SLINKY SPEEDSTERS

Bounce! The ferret leaps and loops across the open prairie in the dark.

Black-footed ferrets move with a bouncy, looping run. Their back curves up and down as they go. This bounding gait looks funny but covers ground fast.

Their flexible spine is the secret. It bends and stretches with every stride. This also lets them twist through tight underground tunnels.

Ferrets can turn around inside a space barely bigger than their own body. They can also run backward quickly when they need to back out of a dead-end tunnel. Every move is built for life underground.

SLEEPY DAYS BUSY NIGHTS

Yawn! The ferret blinks at the setting sun. It is almost time to head out to hunt!

Black-footed ferrets are **nocturnal**. They sleep through most of the day deep inside their burrows. At night, they come out to hunt.

Each ferret patrols a large **territory** night after night. In winter, food grows scarce and they may go days without leaving the burrow, living off stored fat until warmer nights return.

In spring, everything changes. More prey surfaces and mating season begins. Ferrets roam further than ever, driven by hunger and the search for a partner.

SPRING SIGNALS

Male black-footed ferrets use scent to mark their territory and signal to females.

Sniff! A male ferret follows a trail of scent across the dark prairie. He is looking for a mate.

Black-footed ferrets mate in March and April. Longer, warmer nights tell their bodies it is time. Males travel far each night to find a female.

Ferrets live alone most of the year. During mating season, a male visits many female territories. After mating, he moves on. The female raises the kits by herself.

About 41 to 43 days after mating, the kits are born. Most litters have three or four babies. The timing is set so the kits are born in May or June, when food is plentiful.

TINY KITS

FUN
FACT!
Black-footed ferret kits grow so
fast they are nearly full-sized by
the end of their first summer!

30

Squeak! Deep underground, young kits snuggle together to stay warm.

Baby black-footed ferrets are called kits. They are born in May or June inside a prairie dog burrow. A litter usually has three to four kits.

Newborn kits are very small. They weigh only about 0.2 to 0.3 ounces at birth. That is less than a small coin.

Kits are born with their eyes and ears sealed shut. They have a thin coat of white hair. Their dark markings appear around three weeks of age. Their eyes open about 35 days after birth.

LEARNING TO HUNT

DID YOU KNOW?

A mother black-footed ferret carries her kits in her mouth to move them to safety.

Pounce! A young ferret leaps toward its sibling. It is learning the skills it will need to survive.

Mother ferrets raise their kits alone. They feed, clean, and protect the babies underground. Father ferrets do not help raise the young.

Kits drink their mother's milk for about six weeks. Then they begin eating meat. By late summer, the young ferrets start following their mother on real hunts.

They practice by wrestling with their siblings. They watch their mother and copy her moves. By fall, each young ferret must hunt on its own. Their survival through winter depends on what they have learned.

MEET THE FAMILY

European
Polecat

Siberian
Polecat

Sniff! Halfway around the world, two more wild ferret cousins are on the hunt.

Black-footed ferrets have two wild cousins. The European polecat lives in forests and wetlands across Europe. It has dark brown fur with pale patches and a bold face mask. It hunts rabbits, mice, frogs, and birds at night. All pet ferrets in the world are descended from this animal.

The Siberian polecat (also known as the Steppe Polecat) lives on the dry grasslands of Central Asia, from Europe to China. It is pale yellow with dark legs and a dark face mask. Like its North American cousin, it hunts burrowing rodents to survive.

FERRET FRIENDS

Pet ferrets do a happy jump called the weasel war dance. They leap and bounce sideways when excited!

Dook! A pet ferret bounces sideways across the living room in pure joy.

Pet ferrets are not wild animals. They are descended from the European polecat. People have kept them for about 2,500 years.

Unlike wild black-footed ferrets, pet ferrets are very social. They love people and other ferrets.

Pet ferrets need good care every day. They need fresh water, meat-based food, a large cage, and at least four hours of play time. With proper care, they can live 5 to 10 years. A pet ferret is a big, fun responsibility.

SAVING FERRETS

Scientists have begun cloning black-footed ferrets to bring back lost genes!

Click! A scientist's spotlight finds two glowing eyes in the dark prairie. A ferret — alive!

Black-footed ferrets came back from the edge of extinction because people refused to give up. Scientists, ranchers, and wildlife workers all played a part. Today, about 300 ferrets live across 30 protected sites — and that number keeps growing.

The biggest battle ahead is sylvatic plague. This disease can wipe out entire prairie dog towns overnight. Scientists are working on a vaccine, and early results look promising. Every ferret alive today is proof that saving a species is possible.

GLOSSARY

burrow

An underground tunnel and room system where animals live and raise their young.

carnivore

An animal that eats only meat.

nocturnal

Active at night instead of during the day.

musk

A strong-smelling liquid released from a gland near the tail.

territory

An area an animal claims and regularly travels through to find food and mates.